T0036104

TO:

FROM:

PRAISE FOR
MAURA NEVEL THOMAS

"[Empowered Productivity] has transformed my routine and reinvigorated me!"
—Jeff DeLaet, Senior Vice President, T&M Associates

"I have been using the principles from [Empowered Productivity] and I have found so much more time in my day!"
—Dana Garaventa, Human Resources Manager,
Opus One Winery

"I am loving using [Maura's] system! What a difference it makes to finally feel I am controlling my day instead of my day controlling me."
—Rainee Busby, CEO, Fokal Fusion

"[The Empowered Productivity] system gives me so much peace of mind as a business owner, it's incredible!"
—Jason Harden, CEO, Pacific Eagle Electric

"I had no idea [Empowered Productivity] was going to be so life-changing for me."
—Sarah Remmert, Manager, University of
Texas San Antonio

"[Empowered Productivity] has quite frankly been a true 'game-changer' for me in terms of managing my day and freeing me from distractions. This has truly changed my mindset and is beginning to change my behaviors (and habits) for the better."
—Brad Osborne, Senior Quality Manager,
Senior Metal Bellows

FROM
TO-DO
TO
DONE

HOW TO GO FROM BUSY TO PRODUCTIVE BY MASTERING YOUR TO-DO LIST

MAURA NEVEL THOMAS

Copyright © 2021 by Maura Thomas
Cover and internal design © 2021 by Sourcebooks
Cover design by Lindsey Cleworth
Internal images © end sheets, SpicyTruffel/Shutterstock; page vi, Miss Pearl/Getty Images; page x, shironosov/Getty Images; page xvii, AleksandarNakic/Getty Images; page xx, Tetra Images/Getty Images; pages 5 and 90, Image Source/Getty Images; pages 12 and 21, Twomeows/Getty Images; page 26, jayk7/Getty Images; page 33, ExperienceInteriors/Getty Images; page 39, SDI Productions/Getty Images; page 42, Moyo Studio/Getty Images; page 45, © eleonora galli/Getty Images; pages 46 and 63, Westend61/Getty Images; pages 47-48, mything/Shutterstock; pages 70 and 78, 10'000 Hours/Getty Images; page 73, Nora Carol Photography/Getty Images; page 85, Jacobs Stock Photography Ltd/Getty Images; page 94, Warchi/Getty Images; page 100, yacobchuk/Getty Images; page 106, Aurelie and Morgan David de Lossy/Getty Images; page 112, Francesco Bergamaschi/Getty Images; page 118, Paige Cody/Getty Images

Sourcebooks, Simple Truths, and the colophon are registered trademarks of Sourcebooks.

All rights reserved. No part of this book may be reproduced in any form or by any electronic or mechanical means including information storage and retrieval systems—except in the case of brief quotations embodied in critical articles or reviews—without permission in writing from its publisher, Sourcebooks.

This publication is designed to provide accurate and authoritative information in regard to the subject matter covered. It is sold with the understanding that the publisher is not engaged in rendering legal, accounting, or other professional service. If legal advice or other expert assistance is required, the services of a competent professional person should be sought.—*From a Declaration of Principles Jointly Adopted by a Committee of the American Bar Association and a Committee of Publishers and Associations*

All brand names and product names used in this book are trademarks, registered trademarks, or trade names of their respective holders. Sourcebooks is not associated with any product or vendor in this book.

Published by Simple Truths, an imprint of Sourcebooks
P.O. Box 4410, Naperville, Illinois 60567-4410
(630) 961-3900

Printed and bound in China.
OGP 10 9 8 7 6 5 4 3 2 1

This book might not have been possible without the time I spent in my twenties at Time/Design in West Springfield, Massachusetts. During those eight years, I learned a lot about productivity and also a lot about life, business, and myself. In addition to knowledge, I gained there what has become a lifetime friendship. This book is dedicated to Doreen. Thank you for the partnership back then and all the Doritos, pumpkins, support, tears, laughter, and friendship since.

TABLE OF

CONTENTS

THE EMPOWERED PRODUCTIVITY SERIES

My first book, *Personal Productivity Secrets* (Wiley, 2012), was the first published work detailing my Empowered Productivity system which I had been delivering to clients for many years.

Since then, the world of work has continued to evolve. It has left the confines of the office. I write this now in quarantine because of the global COVID-19 pandemic. "Knowledge workers" are required to be more creative, more innovative, and more disruptive, yet with less and less time and space to marshal resources in a thoughtful way because of the countless and increasing demands on our attention.

In the decade since I wrote that book, I've been honored to work with some of the world's most influential leaders and brands. That experience has both refined my thinking and given me the opportunity to defend it in some of the country's most prestigious business outlets. The result is the latest evolution of the Empowered Productivity system, which has been put through much more rigorous testing and refining, incorporating input and feedback from over forty thousand professionals.

This book, detailing action management, is the second in the Empowered Productivity series from Ignite Reads, after *Attention Management: How to Create Success and Gain Productivity—Every Day* published in 2019.

Future planned books in the series will explore communication management and culture change management (for organizational leadership).

I'm confident that the latest version of my Empowered Productivity system, as presented in this series, is the best it's ever been. I'm excited and humbled to join you on your journey to peak productivity and to help empower your ability to achieve the results that are most significant to you, personally and professionally. I'm excited to see the results as more and more people like you can bring **your** unique gifts to the world in a way that inspires, motivates, and excites you rather than exhausts, overwhelms, and stresses you.

INTRODUCTION

PREPARE FOR PRODUCTIVITY

Have you gone to work determined to complete just one or two really important things? But then, before you know it, it's the end of the day and you haven't even had to time to think about those tasks?

Now consider another common scenario: Have you ever reflected around New Year's Day or your birthday that another year has gone by and you've made little or no progress toward getting that promotion—or going back to school, starting that side business, or achieving another life goal you set? Or have you maybe had a friend on your mind, but you realize it's been forever since you've spoken with them?

The two situations are deeply related. If you spend the best part of your days focused on trying to keep up with what the world throws your way, you lose your ability to shape the life you want to live.

True productivity isn't about checking more things off your to-do list every day. It's not about being busy reacting to the unrelenting amount of communication and information you receive every day.

Instead, I believe the pursuit of productivity empowers us to choose our answers to two questions: "What kind of person do you want to be?" and "What kind of life do you want to live?" I define productivity as accomplishing more of what's important to you—what I refer to as your *significant results*.

We all wear many hats in our lives. Not only are we professionals and colleagues, but we are also likely some combination of partner, spouse, parent, child, sibling, aunt, uncle, niece, nephew, friend, neighbor, community member, volunteer, global citizen, and more. And in each of these roles that we play, we have dozens, hundreds, maybe thousands of actions, tasks, and responsibilities that we need to manage in order to be the kind of person we want to be in all parts of our lives. For example, we aren't likely to find it acceptable to be a great colleague but a mediocre parent. Or to be a great partner but an unreliable friend. But holding ourselves to these high standards in all parts of our lives is not only hard, it can also be exhausting, overwhelming, and stressful.

So what then is the solution? Harnessing our time, our to-do list, and our **productivity**.

Productivity is not some innate talent. It's a skill you can learn and practice like any other. Before you decide where you want to go with this book, it helps to understand where you are now with your productivity—your ability to achieve your most significant results.

I generally see three different stages of productivity in my clients:

STAGE ONE:
Busy but Not Productive

Have you ever had a day fly by in a flurry of activity—but leave you unsure at the end whether you really accomplished anything? We all have days like this sometimes. But if you're in Stage One productivity, almost *all* of your days fit this description. When you're at Stage One productivity, you stay primarily in a reactive mode (or if you read the first book in the series, *Attention Management*, you're in the Reactive and Distracted quadrant). This means that dealing with other people and other people's goals dominates your day: going to meetings, answering emails, returning phone calls, clearing other communications like instant messages and chat, and putting out fires.

Your job may require you to spend a lot of time being reactive. For example if you're a manager, your job requires you to put your team's goals first, keep your team members on track, ensure they meet deadlines, and help resolve their interpersonal issues.

If, however, you have even one responsibility that doesn't depend on your staff, for which you alone are responsible, and it cannot be delegated, then you must find some time to be proactive in order to get that project or task done. However, you'll have a hard time doing that if you're stuck in Stage One productivity. This stage is often characterized by long work hours because you may spend your days dealing with others and spend your evenings and weekends getting your own work done (or the reverse). Stage One productivity is often a step on the path to burnout.

STAGE TWO:
Claiming Proactive Time

In Stage Two productivity, you make time daily to be proactive. You regularly knock things off your to-do list, and you finish each workday with at least some sense of accomplishment—that is, during your normal work day, you actually completed some of the tasks that were most important to **you**, so you could feel good about using your evening to disconnect from work.

While this is a great place to be, you may also recognize that you never have the opportunity to collect your thoughts, plan ahead, and be strategic. And this frustrates you because it's standing in the way of the success you know you could achieve. You've got ideas that you are excited to pursue but months go by, and you haven't made much progress. Perhaps you think, *If I only had more time.* But you have the same twenty-four hours in a day that everyone else gets. Traditional time management techniques you've learned in the past dictate that you make appointments with yourself on your calendar. But you find yourself regularly breaking those appointments and dragging them over and over to the next day or the next week on your calendar. This is an indicator that your life is a little too complex to use just a calendar to manage it. You need a more comprehensive system.

STAGE THREE:

Moving Steadily Toward Your Goals

You'll know you're at Stage Three productivity when these two things happen:

1 You accomplish more of the important things each day that move you closer to your major goals or initiatives.

2 You regularly take time to think, to plan, and to marshal your creativity and your unique set of talents, skills, and abilities to get an edge in your work and your life.

Which stage sounds the most like you now? How would moving to the next stage of productivity make your life better? Make a note about where you are currently so that you can see how much you change as you read this book and become more empowered over your productivity—your ability to achieve more of your most significant results.

I don't teach people about productivity because I believe that zero messages in your inbox is the ultimate be-all, end-all, or that there's any inherent virtue in trying to stuff even more activities into our already jam-packed days. I do what I do because I'm passionate about helping others live their lives by design, and be the kind of people they want to be, in all parts of their lives. The techniques you'll learn here have helped countless other busy people do more meaningful work, accomplish more of their goals, and be more present for the important people in their lives.

You can feel the same freedom too. You can take back your days from distractions and other people's priorities.

Flip the page to begin!

ONE

MANAGE YOUR ACTIONS

▬▬▬▬▬▬▬▬▬▬▬

While life is, of course, full of **external** distractions, we also have to deal with **internal** distractions before we can become truly productive. In fact, *you* are the person who interrupts yourself the most. Much of your mental chatter likely includes running down your to-do list all day, trying not to forget anything that's on your plate. Most people write things down to help them remember, and every time we write things on a list somewhere, we tell our brains, "Don't forget." And your brain doesn't know the appropriate time to remind you of all of these things, so it reminds you all the time. In my experience in fact, most people's thoughts, especially at work, are about mentally reviewing things that need to be done.

This effort to remember everything creates a burden on your brain. We only have a certain amount of brainpower available to us at any moment (called our *cognitive capacity*). If some of that cognitive capacity is taken up by trying to remember things we need to do, personally and professionally, then we won't be able to apply ourselves fully (what I call "unleashing our genius") on those important tasks, moments, and interactions that produce the most satisfaction, joy, and impact for our lives.

Instead of writing things down to help you remember, the action management portion of the Empowered Productivity series provides a collection of habits and behaviors for storing, organizing, prioritizing, and *accomplishing* more of your tasks, responsibilities, projects, and commitments—professional and personal—so that you can achieve more of those significant results with less stress and greater efficiency.

But to understand how to achieve these results, we first need to talk about lions…

Why It's Hard to Get Important Work Done (The Lion Syndrome)

If you've ever seen a lion tamer at work—in a movie, on TV, at a circus, or a Vegas show—I bet you didn't realize there was a hidden productivity lesson in the performance.

You might remember that lion tamers take a chair or a stool into the lion's cage with them. A lot of people assume that the chair serves as protection or even a weapon against the lion. It actually has a less obvious use for the tamer. The tamer holds the chair or stool by the seat, and points the legs outward. According to legend, this causes the lion to try to focus on all of the legs at the same time. Doing this is confusing and distracting, and as a result, the lion gets passive and retreats.

3

Whoa! We can imagine the poor lion thinking, *Four different attackers! I've got a lot going on here. I don't know what to do.*

This phenomenon happens to people too. I call it the Lion Syndrome. It's another way of describing Stage One productivity (detailed on page xiv): You have a lot on your mind that you want to get done. Then you arrive at the office to a full inbox, a ringing phone, and a few text message alerts just for good measure. At least three people have asked you if have a minute to talk before you even get to your desk.

Like the lion, you probably feel like retreating when so much is going on. With things coming at you from all directions, it's a waste of time to have to sit down at your desk and wonder, *What do I need to do first?* For most people, the sheer number of potential answers to that question is completely overwhelming.

The most common response for a lot of people when they get overwhelmed like this is to retreat into email. Sure, email makes you feel like you're getting

4

things accomplished. But it's actually a way to be busy but not truly productive. And, over the long term, if you consistently default to email, everything just starts to pile up, and your most important work either doesn't get done or is only done in crisis mode right before it's due. This is an example of getting **trapped by reactivity**.

You are one confused lion. But there's a better way to work.

Action Management

To avoid being overwhelmed by the Lion Syndrome, you need a strategy for the way you approach your work—a way to absorb everything coming at you: all manner of commitments, communication, and information— sort out what matters, and prioritize appropriately. This is where **action management** in the Empowered Productivity system becomes important.

Think of your actions as all of those items on your to-do list; all of those tasks you need or want to get done in all parts of your life. In this book, I'll give you specific steps to immediately regain control of your actions.

My guess is that you're reading this book because you have a busy life, and I bet that busy life is by *choice*. It's busy because you are ambitious and driven, and you have a lot going on. That's great! But what I want for you is to be able to manage that busy life so that it brings you joy and exhilaration, not stress and anxiety.

The Puzzle Strategy

A great way to understand the need for action management is to consider the last time you worked on a puzzle. The first things you probably do are open the puzzle box, dump out all the pieces, and then turn them all face up.

Think about the next thing you do. Most people will identify the edge and corner and assemble those first. If you think about why we all do it this way, it's because it makes sense. It gives you:

- **Perspective**—*a frame that outlines the puzzle and shows you how big it is.*
- **Context**—*giving you a clue as to how the pieces will relate to each other.*
- **A starting point**—*the straight edges offer a clue to where those pieces go.*
- **A quick win**—*you've already been able to make some progress on the project.*

Now imagine that you and I were going to do a puzzle together on your dining room table, but after we dumped the pieces out of the box, I scooped up a bunch at random and carried them into the kitchen, dropped them on the counter, and left them there. Then I scooped up two more bunches and left one on your bed and one on your coffee table. Then I joined you back at the dining room table and suggested we start the puzzle.

My guess is that you'd think I was crazy! You know that having the pieces scattered in various rooms of the house is *not* a smart way to do the puzzle. I'd like to ask you to pause for a minute and think about *why* exactly this isn't a smart strategy for puzzle assembly. Take a minute and jot your ideas down on a piece of paper. Thinking about this before moving on will help you really understand and internalize the point I'm about to make, so do pause and think about it now.

I bet you came up with several reasons, including the following:

- **It's disorganized**—*you wouldn't know where to start, and some of the pieces could get lost without you even realizing it.*

- **It prevents context**—*you can't make sense of how the pieces relate to each other when they aren't all together.*

- **It's inefficient**—*you'd spend a whole lot of time running from room to room looking for the pieces you need and expending unnecessary effort.*

- **It's mentally taxing**—*while you're off looking for the piece you need, you have to remember the shape you're trying to fit. A bump on the left or right?*

- **It's distracting**—*looking for a piece in the kitchen might make you think about making a cup of coffee or dinner, and once you start on one of those, the puzzle gets forgotten.*

- *It's frustrating*—*everything about putting the puzzle together takes longer than it should.*

Now consider that puzzle is your life: Each piece is an action, task, or responsibility, and the rooms of your house represent the way you probably manage those actions now. The kitchen represents a list you've made on paper. The bedroom represents all of those things in your brain that you haven't written down yet. The living room represents all of those flagged emails in your inbox. And in addition to all of those rooms, if you're like most people, you probably have even more rooms where your puzzle pieces live such as sticky notes, one or more apps in your phone, a dry-erase board in your office, appointments with yourself in your calendar, plus all the places at home you're keeping track of your personal tasks.

For all of the same reasons that your puzzle strategy doesn't include scattering pieces all over your house, your strategy for managing your actions shouldn't include storing your tasks in a variety of different places. To manage your life efficiently, you need to be able to accomplish the following:

- ▶ Tackle important work.

- ▶ Prevent things from falling through the cracks.

- ▶ Be judicious with your time.

- ▶ Prioritize effectively.

- ▶ Create realistic timelines for projects.

- ▶ Stay focused.

- ▶ Prevent yourself from overcommitting.

- ▶ Make informed decisions about how and where to direct your time and attention.

All of these things are difficult or impossible without a similar strategy you use for the puzzle—all of the actions stored in one convenient place that is conducive to their organization, categorization, and prioritization.

Otherwise, you are ultimately depending on your memory. Isn't it true that you write things down to help you remember? So we make lists of the things we need to do, and we frequently review our lists to ensure we don't forget anything that needs to get done. But

that's like trying to remember each individual puzzle piece in every room of the house!

Also, when we depend on our memory like that, it's stressful. It takes up brainpower to remember all of those things. Brainpower that could otherwise be used to unleash your genius.

Everything in One Place

Just as the first step of your puzzle strategy would be to gather all the pieces back onto the dining room table, the same is true for your action management strategy. You need to collect all of those tasks into one place.

You may have heard some time management advice that you should only write down your three most important tasks for the day because otherwise your list becomes overwhelming. But without the rest of your list for context, how do you know what the three most important things are?

Before you can organize and prioritize your actions, you need to get *all of them* in one place. You may be reluctant to do this at first because you know that if you really collect all of your actions—personally and professionally—you'll end up with an overwhelming list. Don't worry, we'll address ways to solve that problem later. Also consider this: Even if you had a five-thousand-piece puzzle, you'd still have to have *all* the pieces together in order to get started.

Round Up Your Responsibilities: Two Ways to Get Started

Remember in this puzzle analogy that the puzzle pieces are all of your responsibilities, actions, tasks, projects…everything you need or want to get done in all parts of your life. One of the places that those things are lurking in is your mind. But the truth is **you can only manage what you can see, and you can only see what is outside of your head.** So we need to pull those things out of your brain and also collect all of the other responsibilities that have been hiding in your inbox, various to-do lists, sticky notes, etc.

This process is called a **brain dump**.

"The Whole Enchilada"— A Thorough Brain Dump

The ultimate goal of a thorough brain dump is to clear your mind of *all* of the undone things that are lurking in your brain, randomly distracting you. When you implement the action management portion of the Empowered Productivity system, it means you'll never again have to rely on your memory to keep your life running smoothly. Einstein was thought to believe that we should never memorize anything that we can look up. Relying on your system relieves the burden on your brain of remembering everything, and frees it up to do higher-level activities like innovating and problem solving. My clients report that this transfer from their brain to their system of the dozens, hundreds, or thousands of things they need to keep track of makes them feel like a weight is lifted, and their stress goes way down.

This thorough brain dump does take a while, as we need to address "the whole enchilada." However, if you are willing to take the time upfront, I think you'll find this exercise cathartic, and it will get all your puzzle pieces set up for success. If you don't have time for this, there is another option in the next section.

You'll need a clean sheet of paper and a pen or a blank document on your computer. (If you're using your computer, just be sure to turn off your internet access and close all other windows so you can work uninterrupted.)

Now start listing all the things you've been wanting to do, needing to do, thinking about, stressing over, or trying not to forget—from both your professional life and your personal life. Write down all the stuff that's swirling in your brain, distracting you, maybe even keeping you up at night.

Don't censor yourself. If something is on your mind, just write it down. Put each item on a separate line, but don't try to organize your list any further. The important thing right now is just getting all this stuff recorded somewhere outside your brain. Ideally you'll get into a flow of *dumping*, and the ideas will stream out. That's why you should do this on a blank document at first. Trying to figure out how each item relates to your system will prevent the flow.

If you're feeling a little stalled, here are a few prompts to jog your thinking:

- *What projects do you have going on right now, both at work and at home?*
- *Look around your work space (or, if you're not in your work space, call up a mental image). Do you see any reminders of things you need to do?*
- *Do the same exercise with your home. Do you notice any reminders of things you would like to do or projects that you need to finish?*
- *What do you need to plan in your professional or personal life? This could include events, presentations, celebrations…you name it.*

▸ *Do you have any personal or business travel coming up? Is there anything you need to do related to these trips? Have you nailed down all the details, like your rental car?*

▸ *Does your company have new initiatives going on that you need some time to step back and think about?*

▸ *Do you need to send any gifts, cards, thank-you notes, or emails? (Not counting all of the messages currently in your inbox, awaiting a reply. We'll get to those later.)*

▸ *Think about the different departments in your company and the different people you work with. Are there any outstanding issues or questions you need to resolve?*

▸ *Is anything you own due for repair or maintenance?*

▸ *How about your kids? Do they need anything for school or their extracurricular activities?*

▸ *Do you have any outstanding volunteer responsibilities?*

▸ *Are your pets due for a vet checkup or a medicine refill?*

For a "Brain Dump Prompt List" document that

you can download as a PDF, and an audio version that you can listen to, visit maurathomas.com/braindump.

Once you feel confident that everything is out of your brain, it's time to collect tasks and responsibilities from the other places you have them recorded. You can physically put them together with other paper lists you have or hand-copy them onto the same list. If you're doing your brain dump digitally, you can copy and paste from other documents or scan them as images into the document. It doesn't really matter, as long as everything is physically together. Some places to check include:

- *Any appointments you've made with yourself to get tasks done or appointments on calendars you use in your work and personal life. Add these tasks to your brain dump list. (Actual appointments with other people stay on your calendar.)*
- *Combine any other to-do lists you have with your brain dump list.*

▸ *Go through any notebooks where you keep notes from meetings and add any tasks from there to your brain dump list.*

▸ *Collect any sticky notes or other papers that have tasks on them and add those to your brain dump list.*

▸ *Go through the papers on your desk and in the stack of mail and paperwork at home and add any tasks to your brain dump list that immediately jump out at you. If this is a daunting task, you can add "Go through the mail" (for example) as an item on your brain dump list.*

Got everything together? If you're like a lot of people I've worked with, you're feeling a sense of relief right now that you've collected everything. My client, Jonathan Davis, once said, **"Until you do this, you can't truly appreciate all the benefits of clearing your mind."** But many of my clients say that, simultaneous with that sense of relief, they also feel a little overwhelmed by everything that's on their plate.

Don't worry, that tension won't last. Now that you can see all that you have to do, you can start managing it more effectively.

Quick Start Brain Dump

I don't want you to feel like getting started with the Empowered Productivity system is a daunting task, so if the process above makes you feel overwhelmed, or if you can't carve out enough time to do it properly, there's a "shortcut" that will allow you to jump right in.

Still start with that same blank paper and pen, or the blank document on your computer, but just take 5–10 minutes and jot down the most pressing dozen or so things on your mind right now. Set the timer for maybe 10 minutes, and just write down everything you can think of that you need to get done—personally or professionally—until the timer goes off. Whatever you come up with should be enough to get you started.

The Five Ways to Organize

During your brain dump, we rounded up all your *stuff*—your tasks, commitments, responsibilities, and everything else on your mind—and got it all in one place. Now it's time to get it in order. So what's the best way to do that? According to Richard Saul Wurman, the author of *Information Anxiety*, there are essentially five ways to organize everything in your life. You're likely using all of them, but the final two, in particular, will play important roles in becoming more productive and organizing your newly assembled pile of tasks.

1. **Organizing Alphabetically:** Alphabetical organization is useful for things like files, lists, and reference information, such as your contacts.

2. **Organizing by Size:** Arranging things smallest to largest is useful for organizing physical items. For example, you might keep books on your bookshelf starting with the largest on the left down to the

smallest on the far right. Similarly a warehouse might store large inventory in one area and smaller parts in a separate section.

3 **Organizing by Location:** If you keep all the items to take with you when you leave the house (keys, wallet, phone, etc.) near the door, that's organizing by location. Organizing by location is also useful at work. For example, maybe you keep information on international clients and domestic clients in different folders on your computer.

4 **Organizing by Time:** A calendar is a tool for organizing by time and this is, of course, useful for managing time-based commitments.

5 **Organizing by Category:** This is the secret to making your brain dump less overwhelming and by far the most helpful, productive, and actionable way to organize tasks.

As I noted previously, the final two methods will be the focus for action management. Let's begin by organizing our time.

1 | Tuesday

08.00

09.00

10.00

11.00

12.00

01.00

02.00

03.00

04.00

05.00

06.00

TWO

ORGANIZE YOUR TIME

∎∎∎∎∎∎∎∎∎∎∎∎∎∎∎∎∎∎∎∎∎∎∎∎∎∎∎∎∎∎∎∎

When we're young, we have very little discretionary time—our lives are very time-based: We're told what time to go to school or class; what time the buses come; what days we have to turn in our homework and reports; and what days and times we have to report to after-school work and activities. That's why for most people, their first organization tool is a calendar (maybe the one mom or dad hung on the refrigerator, or the paper planner that helped you keep your assignments straight). However, the problem comes when our tendency to organize by time becomes a habit even after we get out of school, take on more responsibility, and have much more control over our time. Once we reach adulthood (for some people, even in their teens), our lives tend to become far too complex for simple, time-based organization.

If you've been using a calendar as your primary productivity tool, I'm going to suggest you make a big shift. In the Empowered Productivity system, a calendar is used *only* for things that have a **strong relationship to time**—things happening on a certain day, or on a certain day *and* at a certain time.

For example:

▶ Appointments

▶ Meetings

▶ Travel

▶ Birthdays

▶ Events (such as a conference)

Events or tasks that involve someone other than yourself typically have the strongest relationship to time. For example, you might skip a workout to sleep in on Saturday morning, but you probably wouldn't stand up a friend on the racquetball court. Therefore, appointments and commitments with others make perfect sense to manage using a time-based tool (a calendar).

However, as we get older and take on more responsibility, many of the things we need or want to do have a **weak relationship to time.** They don't have a due date, or the due date is some point in the future. These are tasks that you would like to do today, and which you might intend to do today, but there would be no consequences if you did them tomorrow, or the next day, or even later. For example, you have a report due in three weeks, but you could complete it anytime between now and then. Or you need to make a dentist appointment, but it isn't essential that you do so right now, today. If you go back and look at your brain dump,

I bet most of the items on it have a weak relationship to time—you want to do them, they need to get done, but *exactly when* you do them isn't that important.

Making appointments with yourself to complete tasks means that you're using a time-based tool to organize tasks that have a weak relationship to time—causing you to work harder than you need to. Since the first person you will break an appointment with is yourself, you may find yourself rearranging your calendar often. That time you set aside to work on the report gets pushed from today to tomorrow to next Tuesday. And by putting things on your calendar that you'd *like* to do today but don't *have* to do today, you're unnecessarily cluttering your calendar, making your days seem overwhelming.

Now that you understand the most efficient use of your calendar, it's time to review your brain dump list and identify any items that have a strong relationship to time—appointments, meetings, events you are attending, and so forth. Add any of these to your calendar that aren't already there. Resist the urge to add items to your calendar that you would **like** to do on a certain day. Only items that would have consequences, or that you'd have to renegotiate with someone else if you didn't do them, belong on your calendar. Or, again, only items that have a *strong* relationship to time. Whether they are from your professional life or your personal life, I recommend that all of your brain dump items with a strong relationship to time should go on the same calendar (see the upcoming section, Manage One Life, Not Two). In the context of the Empowered Productivity system, I refer to items with a strong relationship to time as "appointments" or "events," and items with a weak relationship to time as "tasks," "action items," or "to-do's."

After all items from your brain dump with a strong relationship to time are recorded on your calendar, highlight each of them off your brain dump list. This signals that they are entered into your system, but you can still read them. On any paper notes, I like highlighting things better than crossing them off. It puts the emphasis on your accomplishments rather than the work still left to do, and we are motivated by accomplishment! Here's a test to see if that's true for you: Do you ever write down something that you've already accomplished, just so you can cross it off?

One of my mentors early in my career referred to her highlighter as her PMD—her personal motivational device! To this day, I still use a highlighter to celebrate accomplishments whenever possible, and any time I have items on paper, I try to get my entire list bright.

Manage One Life, Not Two

As a best practice, you should always use the same tools (like a calendar) to manage your professional responsibilities and commitments as your personal ones. You are most efficient and effective when you treat professional and personal responsibilities as parts of a whole rather than separate things.

Thanks to technology and remote work, the lines

have blurred between work and personal time. You may often find yourself handling work responsibilities on personal time and handling personal responsibilities during work hours. If you're self-employed or a business owner, it's hard to even see the line where your professional life ends and your personal life begins!

So why fight to keep a firm line between the two? Trying to segregate personal from professional means you'll need two calendars (and other tools, which you'll read about later in the book), and this will cause you to work harder to stay in control of everything. It's easier to have all of your appointments on one calendar and all of your tasks on one list.

That said, I do recognize that this isn't possible for everyone. If you work at a company where information is very tightly controlled, highly regulated, or subject to open records laws, you may not feel comfortable storing personal details on your work computer. Only you can make the decision if you should keep two sets of tools or one, but you should make that decision knowing that two creates twice as much work and increases the odds that you will double-book yourself and miss things. If it's feasible for you, you will be more efficient if you can keep everything together in one place.

Make Your Calendar More Ambient

If you're reading this book in a room with windows, you know without having to do anything, whether it's daytime or nighttime. If it's daytime, you also know whether it's sunny or cloudy. You didn't need some alert or notification telling you about the weather, or if the sun is still up. And you don't have to actively go seek out that information either. You just know, thanks to the **ambient information** the window was quietly providing in the background.

Ambient information provides you with data without effort or interruption. This makes it the easiest kind of information to digest and, therefore, the most efficient way to receive information. There are a couple of easy ways to make your calendar more ambient and, therefore, more efficient.

Use Linear View

In most digital calendars, a month view is a block and a week view is linear. You can glean more information at a glance by making linear your default view.

A block calendar displays your appointments on a given day but, without clicking on each appointment, it's difficult to know exactly how much of your day is booked.

A linear view of your calendar gives you much more information. You can tell exactly how much of your time is committed and how much is free with just a glance. The vertical block for each day represents a whole day and the empty spaces give you a quick sense of your unscheduled time for that day.

Color-Coding

Another way to make your calendar information more ambient is to color-code your appointments.

If you glance at the week ahead on your digital calendar and all the appointments are in white, you can discern how many appointments you have, but you don't get any other information about them. By color-coding your appointments, you can get a better sense of what's coming up for you.

The categories you use in your color-coding depend on what's most important for you to know at a glance about each appointment. You could use different colors to identify the following types of events:

- *Meetings you requested vs. meetings that others requested*
- *Meetings at your office vs. those requiring travel*
- *Sales activities vs. marketing activities*
- *Business appointments vs. personal appointments*

Now, with a quick glance at your calendar, different colors denote the type of activity. A quick look at your calendar helps you know what to expect for the week.

Another great reason to color-code your calendar is that it creates a time-use report card that can serve to pat you on the back or get you back on track. For example, if your goal is to spend a certain amount of time per week coaching your direct reports, then assigning a color to those appointments is a great way to quickly see whether the way you are spending your time aligns with that goal.

Time Blocking

I'm often asked about time blocking—or making a calendar appointment with yourself—to accomplish tasks, especially those you've been procrastinating on. Many people try to assign everything they need to do to a time on their calendar. I don't recommend that, since the first person you will break an appointment with is yourself. So I find that people who use their calendar this way spend too much time rearranging their calendar, leaving too little time to accomplish things. Also there is the danger of things falling through the cracks

when you both don't keep the appointment you made with yourself, *and* you forget to move the appointment to another time on your calendar.

There is another activity that I recommend, but don't really consider time-blocking. If other people have access to your calendar to check your availability, block out time every day to protect it from being overrun with meetings. But don't assign specific tasks to yourself during this time. Just use it as time to get work done, such as thinking, email, tasks, or some combination. I call it "proactive time."

However, there *are* times when it can be useful to make an appointment with yourself. Follow these three rules for greatest efficiency:

1 Use time blocking very selectively—only for very important things, and only once in a while. If you do it too often, you'll start breaking those appointments with yourself, and the technique will lose its effectiveness.

2 Don't block your time too far in the future; it's too uncertain. To get important things done, block time on your calendar today or tomorrow. If you schedule too far in advance and your priorities change, you'll end up breaking those appointments with yourself. There's one exception to this: If you have an important project deadline in the future, it's helpful to block some time a day or so before that deadline in order to finish up the project, add final thoughts, or give it a final once-over.

3. Don't make your time blocks too long. It's very difficult to block out a whole day, for example. Focus waxes and wanes. Time blocking works best in blocks of two hours or less. I suggest you start with appointments of one hour or less and see how that works out for you.

THREE

ORGANIZE YOUR TASK LIST

Some items from your brain dump may now have found their way to your calendar. But we still need to give the rest, likely the majority, a home. These are the things you'll tackle in your discretionary time—in other words, in the periods between the appointments on your calendar.

The home for these items is your **task list** or **to-do list**. You may already be using a list of some kind to keep track of some of your responsibilities, whether that's an app on your phone or some notes scribbled on the pad at your desk. But I'm willing to bet that your list could be doing a lot more to boost your productivity than it currently is. I'm going to show you how to create a task list that both helps you identify the best use of your time in any given moment and also inspires you to take action.

Even after putting some items on your calendar, your brain dump list may still be relatively long and quite varied—from making your next dentist appointment to brainstorming ideas for that business you want to start someday, and everything in between. Right now these items might be all jumbled up together, or on multiple different lists. If you had, say, twenty minutes to try to get something done using one or more long, disorganized list, you'd use up a lot of that time just trying to figure out what to do next.

To make it useful, we need to bring some order to your list. But what's the best way to do that?

Think back to the five ways to organize we talked

about on page 23. The method that's most effective for managing your task list is **organizing by category**. This isn't an arbitrary choice. Organizing your list by category will help you to be more productive and efficient.

Why is that? Because your brain *loves* categories. It takes less time and effort to process categorized information versus uncategorized information. Even if you've never considered this consciously, I think it's something we all know intuitively. As with the puzzle strategy, if you've ever started working a complicated jigsaw puzzle by separating the pieces into types (for example, edge pieces, water pieces, building pieces, and grass pieces), then you already have some experience organizing things by category.

Categorical Organization— The Fruit Test

The best way I know to explain the power of categorizing is to show you an exercise I share with participants in my productivity training engagements with corporate clients.

When you look at the image below, note how long it takes you to determine two things:

1. How many different types of fruit are there?
2. Which fruit is there more of?

Now go through the same process with this image:

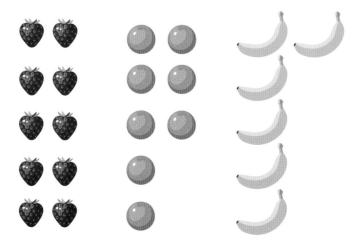

As you've seen, it's *a lot* easier and faster to answer the two questions using the second image than it is with the first.

The same thing is true with your task list. When it's uncategorized, you spend too much time and energy figuring out what needs to be done before you can even *do* anything. After we divide your list into categories, everything is going to feel much more manageable and actionable.

Categories That DON'T Work

You can't use just any categories for your list, though. In fact, some ways we've been taught to categorize our responsibilities are just not effective:

- **Business and personal** *are not helpful categories because many people do personal tasks at work and vice versa. Small business owners often have an exceptionally difficult time distinguishing between business and personal. (See Manage One Life, Not Two, page 32)*

- *Categorizing tasks as* **urgent or not urgent** *is similarly ineffective because your priorities change so quickly that you would be constantly reorganizing your list.*

- *Many people categorize their work using a priority system such as* **ABC** *(or 123 or High-Low-Medium), assuming that this will quickly help them decide what needs to be done next. Unfortunately, chances are good that everything you write down is important to you. In fact, the main reason you put tasks on your list* *is that they are weighing on your mind, and you don't want to forget them. The things that aren't important don't even make it onto your list. So almost every-thing that does make the list gets the highest prior-ity. If you do happen to assign a lower priority to some items, they never get done unless something happens to make them a higher priority. Prioritizing is useful, but as a secondary layer of organization after categorization.*

The Categories That DO Work

What categories *do* work for your task list? Through decades working in the productivity industry and work with countless clients, I've found that there are seven categories that have proven to be the most useful in helping busy professionals track all of their responsibil-ities and make the best use of their time. And it turns out that these categories are useful for all office staff, from the administrative assistant, to the sales manager, to the CEO and everyone in between. They have also proven to be useful in virtually every industry. They are:

- *Next Actions*
- *Projects*
- *Waiting For*
- *Talk To*

- *Future*
- *Someday/Maybe*
- *Location*

Next Actions

Tasks belong in the **Next Actions** category of your task list if they are single-step, and you have all the information you need to complete them. There is nothing to prevent you from completing a Next Action other than time or opportunity. A few examples:

- *Call tax advisor. (You have the number, the necessary papers, and you know what you need to say.)*
- *Email book club members. (You have their addresses and the subject clearly in mind.)*

▶ *Write the client proposal. (You have already spoken to the client, done your research, and collected your thoughts.)*

A Next Action could be something that's going to take you a minute or two. And it also could be something that's going to take a little longer, maybe five to thirty minutes, like an expense report or editing a document.

In theory a Next Action could also be something that's going to take you a really long time, like an hour or more. But Next Actions that feel difficult and time-consuming pose a problem: We are more likely to procrastinate on them.

Most people (me included!) tend to gravitate toward the fast and easy things on our to-do list and leave the ones that sound big and hard until later. But those seemingly difficult and time-consuming tasks are also likely to be the ones that are most satisfying.

For example, when writing books, I submit the first

draft of the completed manuscript to my publisher, and it feels great! But at some point in the future, they send it back to me with recommended changes from the editor. And so, technically, *Incorporate the edits to complete the next draft of the book* is a Next Action because I have all the information I need to complete it. But incorporating someone else's edits, especially for an entire book, is difficult, time-consuming work, and completing the next round of the book is going to take me hours and hours. So if I write the Next Action that way on my list, it is going to feel overwhelming, and therefore I would be tempted to skip over it and pick something faster and easier. (In other words, I would procrastinate!)

But this Next Action is among the most important on my list! So to overcome procrastination on these difficult, time-consuming Next Actions, break them down by finding (or creating) a natural stopping point. For example, instead of writing, *Incorporate the edits*, I would write *Incorporate the edits for thirty minutes*, and I would set a timer.

Or I could write *Incorporate the edits of the first ten pages*, or *...of chapter one*. Since we tend to gravitate toward the fast and easy things on our list, we need to make *everything* sound fast and easy! *Natural stopping points* is the first technique that we can use to our advantage. But maybe thirty minutes, ten pages, or a whole chapter doesn't sound *fast and easy* to you. And if that's true, you can shorten your natural stopping point to something that *does* sound fast and easy. But don't make your task too short, because then you won't be able to take advantage of **activation energy**, which will be your best tool for overcoming procrastination.

Activation energy is the energy required to get started, and getting started is always the hardest part of anything. And when it comes to important tasks like getting a book finished, these tasks need some amount of *brainpower momentum.* You've got brainpower momentum when you've put sufficient thought and effort into a task so that the full range of your knowledge, wisdom, experience, passion, diligence, and other mental resources are fully mobilized in the service of that task.

Once we generate some brainpower momentum, we create the activation energy that makes it more likely that we will keep going.

So if *Incorporate the edits for thirty minutes* doesn't sound fast and easy enough, I might shorten the Next Action to ten minutes. But I can't make it too short; for example, two minutes. Because while *Incorporate the edits for two minutes* might sound fast and easy, it isn't enough time to build up brainpower momentum, and therefore I wouldn't get activation energy. By the time I opened the files and began to read the comments and suggested changes from the editor, the time would be up!

So a little more time, like ten or fifteen minutes, still sounds pretty fast and easy, but also is likely to generate the activation energy to keep going for longer. Even if I didn't go beyond the ten minutes, I still got more done than if I had skipped over the item on my list because it sounded too difficult and time-consuming. This avoids any **friction** on your list, which is exactly what it sounds like when compared to activation energy.

If a task sounds hard, or if there's something else standing in the way of us doing that thing, then we are less likely to do it. That thing standing in the way is friction. So continuing the Next Action example of *Incorporate the edits for ten minutes*, let's say those edit files are saved on my computer somewhere, but I forgot where I saved them. So now I realize I don't know where they are, and I'll have to go searching for them before I can complete this Next Action. That's friction, and it makes it more likely that I will skip over that task (procrastinate) when I see it on my list. It doesn't take very much friction to prevent us from doing something.

So to remove the friction, when I put the task on my Next Action list, I would write, *Incorporate the edits for ten minutes, in Documents/Book Files/Edits*. This makes it super easy for me to get started and, therefore, more likely that I'll actually do it.

This idea of removing friction works not only for yourself but others in your life too! Is there anybody else in your life who you wish would do things or not do things, like who coworkers, family members, or kids? Consider how you can remove friction to make things easier or create friction to make things harder, and this is a useful way to influence the behavior of others.

As an example, if you want to eat healthier snacks during the day, put a bowl of nuts on a table that you walk by frequently. Then you'll be more likely to grab a handful of those than to get the cookies out of the cabinet.

As an example for business, I bet you purchase more on Amazon than you used to. One reason is probably because Amazon makes it so easy to purchase from them. There is very little friction—the app is right there on your phone and your credit card and shipping address are stored. All it takes is a couple of taps and the item you need arrives at your door in a day or two.

A Final Note about Next Actions

Some of the tasks on your lists need to happen more than once, but there's an important distinction to keep in mind here. A recurring task is one you simply need a reminder to do periodically. For example, your Next Actions might include filling out an expense report at the end of every month or turning in a time sheet at the end of every week. A habit is a behavior you either automatically practice regularly or that you would like to become automatic. Don't put your established habits on your task list. They'll just clutter it up. If you're trying to form a new habit, go ahead and create a recurring task with a reminder, to help you get started. But also realize that you'll need to take other steps, such as making it fast and easy, removing friction, creating activation energy, and getting specific. Creating good habits and breaking bad ones is actually a process unto itself. Two excellent books that I recommend on this topic are *Atomic Habits* by James Clear and *Smart Change* by Art Markman.

Projects

Some of your Next Actions will be one-offs, but some will be related to larger **Projects**. Projects are big picture activities that you are working on or about to begin. They happen in multiple steps (including Next Actions and items in other categories) over multiple time periods. You usually can't finish a Project in one sitting.

If you're wondering whether something is a Project, a good litmus test is whether it has a definable beginning and end. For example, if you are an attorney, and you also manage employees, *Manage Staff* is not a Project. It is just one of the ongoing aspects of your work because it has no beginning and no end.

Here are a few examples of Projects:

▸ *Plan Mom's birthday party.*

▸ *Develop next quarter's goals.*

▸ *Write a company benefits guide.*

As you label the Projects on your brain dump list,

you'll also probably notice other items on your list that are Next Actions belonging to that Project. If you realize you have a Project with no Next Actions, take a moment to define the *next* thing that has to happen in order to move that Project forward. Projects without Next Actions are unlikely to advance.

A Projects list is useful to help you stay focused on your big picture responsibilities. You've probably heard the expression, *I can't see the forest for the trees*. A Project list ensures that you can always see the forest, that you're continually advancing your big picture initiatives, and that your workload is manageable and realistic. As you did your brain dump, you probably realized that it's not just your daily responsibilities that were weighing on your mind. I bet you wrote down at least a couple of your long-term goals or major aspirations for your life as well.

Getting those goals out of your head is a powerful step toward making them happen. Proponents of positive psychology and the law of attraction will tell you that if you can see and articulate your goals, you can achieve them.

For example, let's say you attended a political rally that inspired you to pursue a new goal: Get elected to public office. But this isn't specific enough, and you may have no idea how to start achieving this goal. To make your goal more actionable, start breaking it down into Projects. Your first project might be something like *Research responsibilities and requirements for local, state, and national elected officials.* Then you would break that Project down into Next Actions, like *Email local party chair (add name and email address) to set up a coffee meeting* or *Do an internet search for a class on running for office.*

When that Project is done, you can launch the next phase of your goal with a new project, like *Run for city council next year.* That Project will have its own set of Next Actions.

You get the idea. This is how the Empowered Productivity system enables you to turn your big dreams into daily actions so that you can make continual progress on what's most important to you. That's what true productivity is all about.

Waiting For

We do a lot of waiting. You send an email and then wait for a reply. You submit a report and then wait for the feedback of everyone who has to weigh in. The Next Actions for these items belong to someone else. But you still have a responsibility, which is to ensure that you don't forget to close the loop, and maybe that you follow up at some point with the appropriate people. Trying to remember everything that you're waiting for without an effective system in place requires a lot of mental effort. By collecting everything you're waiting for in one place that you can consult when you're feeling uneasy, you can reserve your mental energy for more important work.

That's why **Waiting For** is an important category for your task list. When you use it, you can feel assured

that you'll stay on top of any necessary follow-ups if you don't hear back from the people you're waiting on.

Your Waiting For list might include items like these:

- *Hear back from [coworker] about [information] requested by [client name].*
- *Receive [information] from [client name] to start [new assignment] on time.*
- *Receive the sales figures from the sales department to complete month-end reports.*

Talk To

When you have a lot of interaction with someone, personally or professionally, you often think of things to share with that person. When that happens, most people do one of the following:

- *Call, email, or text that person every time they think*

of something, which results in messages back and forth for both of you.

- *Go see that person (if they're nearby) every time they think of something.*
- *Tuck the thought away to share it the next time they see the person.*

The first two options are disrupting, distracting, and inefficient for both you and the other person. The third option puts an unnecessary burden on your brain and probably won't go according to plan anyway.

It's more effective to create a **Talk To** category that includes the people with whom you work closely or communicate with frequently. This list is a way of *batching* communication. As you think of things you need to communicate to a person, create tasks that start with that person's name along with whatever you need to say to them. For example: *Joe: Ask his opinion on the pricing for the client proposal.* Then assign it to your Talk To category.

When you are seeing or speaking with that person anyway, like when you are both attending the same meeting or when you bump into them in the break room, you can refer to your Talk To category to ensure you address those items in a way that isn't distracting or disruptive for either of you. Or you could even schedule a meeting with them to go over everything on your Talk To list. Either way, instead of sending a bunch of different emails they have to deal with or distracting them by dropping by their desk repeatedly, you're covering everything in one conversation. That's much more efficient for both of you, and you're helping your organization run more efficiently as well by cutting down on the overall volume of communication.

Next Action vs. Talk To

+ If you think of something you need to communicate to a person you will *not* likely run into during your regular daily activities, then the item is a Next Action, not a Talk To. Urgency can also affect whether you categorize a communication task as a Talk To or a Next Action. If your knee has been bothering you lately, and you think you should ask about it at your next checkup, that's a Talk To item for your doctor. But if your thoughts are more like, "Oh, man—I *really* messed up my knee at the gym yesterday," then calling the doctor's office to schedule an appointment becomes a Next Action.

Future

Future items are Projects or Next Actions you are definitely going to do—but you're not going to do them *right now or in the immediate future*. Capturing items on your Future list prevents you from forgetting them but keeps your focus in the present. As time goes by, you can capture details related to each Future item in the notes section of the task, so all pertinent information is ready and waiting for you when it comes time to move that item to your Project or Next Actions category.

For example, let's say it's August, and you decide to hire a new project manager in the first quarter of next year. Automatically your mind starts whirring with things you need to do—write the job description, look at the resumes you have on file, and enlist a recruiter. But then you realize it's too soon to do any of that.

So you won't forget these tasks, put an item on your Future list that reads *Hire project manager*. Most digital task managers (we'll get to that later in the book) have a place where you can write notes related to a task. So in your task *Hire project manager*, you can enter in the notes section all those tasks currently on your mind. This allows you to capture them so you don't have to rely on your memory. Then set a reminder on the task for, say, November 10. Now you can feel assured that you'll begin the hiring process at the appropriate time, and you can redirect your mind to other things now. When the reminder goes off, change the category of the task from Future to Projects (denoting that it's active), and pull some of the Next Actions out of the notes section of the task (like *Call the recruiter*) and add them to your Next Actions list.

Someday/Maybe

Someday/Maybe items are ideas that in the moment seem like they have potential, but you aren't committed to acting on them yet. And in fact you may never act on them. A Someday/Maybe list gives you a place

to capture dreams, ambitions, ideas, and so on. Keeping a Someday/Maybe list helps you live purpose-fully: Whether you act on these items at some point depends on your intentional decision, *instead of* on whether you happen to remember them.

Someday/Maybe items are very subjective. For example, I have a running list of things I've learned during my decades as a small business owner. When I share some of them with people I mentor, they always tell me how helpful they are. It occurs to me that writing up these things into an article, or even a book, would be fun and potentially help a lot of new business owners. But this is outside my current area of focus, and I don't really have the time or the inclination to do this any time soon. Still, I think it's a good idea, and I don't want to forget. So it goes on my Someday/Maybe list. But someone else may be starting a consulting company based on their own ideas on this topic, and so writing a series of articles like this is one of their current Projects to get started.

Location

Your Next Actions list should contain only items that you can complete while you are in the physical location where you typically work. For example, if you work at an office outside your home, items on your Next Actions list will be things that you can and will do from your office, whether they are work-related or personal, such as *Call the doctor to make an appointment*. This is personal, but you will probably do it from the office.

However, you will also have some tasks that can only be completed while you are in a specific location other than the one where you typically work. For example, *Replace the lightbulb in the garage*. This is personal, and you can't *do it at work*. Tasks like this should be categorized by the name of the location where you need to complete it. In other words, you won't actually have a category called *Location*, but you will have categories for the locations other than your regular workplace where your tasks happen—Home, Errands, Cleveland Office, etc.

Any time you need to do a specific thing when you're in a particular place—or if there's something you can do *only* in that particular place—it's helpful to have a Location category for it. This helps you remember what you need to accomplish when you're in different locations. But it also helps free up your attention. By taking these tasks off your Next Actions list (which, you'll remember, contains only tasks you can carry out where you work), you ensure that they won't be on your mind when you can't do anything about them.

Here are some examples of how you can use locations as categories:

- **Home**

  Change lightbulb in garage.

  Collect food to donate at soup kitchen.

  Clean filter in HVAC unit.

- **Errands**

  Pick up dry cleaning.

  Return library books.

  Mail packages.

- **Cleveland Office**

  Take sales manager out to lunch.

  Update software on Cleveland server.

  Drop in on Cleveland's top three clients.

In summary, you will create categories in your task manager called:

- *Projects*
- *Next Actions*
- *Talk To*
- *Waiting For*
- *Future*
- *Someday/Maybe*

Instead of a category called "Location," you'll have one or more as in the example above. They could also be temporary locations. For example, if you're going on vacation to San Diego, and you learn about a restaurant you want to try and an activity you want to engage in while you're there, create a temporary list called *San Diego* and capture those items on that list. When you get back from San Diego, you can delete that category.

Now you have an understanding of all the categories. Go through your brain dump list and make a note of the category it belongs to beside each one.

Get Some Help with Your Tasks

Just because a task is on your list doesn't mean *you* have to do that task. If you don't love doing something, and it doesn't require your specific expertise, consider hiring someone to help you. There are many ways to get support in small increments, often for a lot less money than you think. Furthermore, the money you invest in getting help can pay off many times over in reduced stress and more time to work on the things that are most important to you, and that only you can do.

For example, recently I had a Project to *Convert my presentation from Keynote to PowerPoint*. I dreaded doing this, and while I could have muddled through it, I'm not a PowerPoint expert, and it was likely to take me hours to complete. So instead, I created a Next Action to *Hire a presentation expert from Upwork*. It took me about ten minutes to post the Project. Within twenty minutes I had six applicants. I chose one, uploaded the files, and this Project was done the next day for about $100. I considered this a much better use of my resources.

Any Leftovers?

Are there any tasks that didn't fit in any of your task categories or find a home on your calendar? Chances are these items are actually notes. Notes are reference materials that don't currently require action. Notes can be things like ideas (I keep a running list of ideas for articles), instructions (I never remember how to create an out-of-office message on my email, so I have a note with those step-by-step instructions), and lists (books I want to read, movies I want to see). Creating a notes section for yourself can be a fantastic tool to create more time for yourself—often just by simply eliminating the mental clutter holding on to these ideas can cost us.

FOUR

MAKE THINGS EASY FOR YOUR "DOER"

When it comes down to it, **taking action** is what your list—and the action management portion of the Empowered Productivity system—is all about. Right now, as we work on setting up your list, your inner planner is active. However, it's your inner doer who'll be using the list. Many of us love utilizing our inner planner. Our planner has all these great intentions and ideas and relishes in listing them out and putting them in order. However, we also need to motivate our inner doer to accomplish the mission the planner sets forth.

Otherwise our list is meaningless. You could have the most brilliant plans and ideas in the world, but they only matter if you manifest them as actions. Your planner needs to guide your doer in a very specific way in order to inspire action.

I want you to picture being in doer mode and using your list during a typical day at work. You're going to be busy and moving quickly. And things will likely be hectic around you. Your opportunities to get things done often occur in very short windows—like a few minutes between meetings or before everyone else arrives in the morning. To empower your productivity, your list needs to help you quickly identify the best use of your time in those stray moments so you can take *immediate* action in the most appropriate way, based on your priorities.

So let's say you look at your list and see an item that just reads *Budget*.

Your planner knew what you meant when you wrote *Budget*. You thought it was clear what that word entailed. But when you're in doer mode trying to use the list amid your stressful day, you have a different reaction.

Budget sounds big and hard.

It sounds like it's going to take a long time.

And just reading the word *Budget* doesn't make clear what you need to do in that moment to accomplish that task.

All of that makes it likely you'll just skip over *Budget* when you see it on your list.

Budget becomes a **speed bump** on your list. It makes you slow down to consider just exactly you meant by *Budget*. In other words, it creates friction. And just as you do with a speed bump on the road when you're driving, when you come across a speed bump on your list, you're likely to just go around it, and pick something on your list that sounds faster and easier. But getting that budget done might just be one of the most important things on your plate right now, and if you keep skipping over it, you're going to find yourself under pressure, trying to get it done at the last minute. That's not the way to produce your best work.

So when you add items into your task manager, it's important to phrase each item in a way that keeps it from becoming a speed bump. When you're in doer mode, you need to know *exactly* how to act on an item when you see it on your list, without having to stop and think.

That means being super specific in how you record each task. Don't use personal shorthand or assume that you'll know what it means when you see it. That's just creating a speed bump for your doer.

To see what I mean, compare the two columns below. One uses shorthand for Next Actions. The other spells out specifically what needs to be done:

▸ **Before**

Expense report

Kelly—budget?

Deal with the study

Bday card

▸ **After**

Enter receipts in the envelope from Chicago trip
into spreadsheet.

Email Kelly for her budget numbers.

Put a link to the study on the website.

Look up address to mail Karen's birthday card.

See how much easier the tasks in the After column seem compared to the Before column? Your doer should be ready to dive in!

You'll also be helping your doer a lot by starting each item on your list with an **action verb**. Now, some words are not as actionable as others. For example, let's consider words that might come up a lot in your responsibilities: words like *organize, plan, develop, implement, and follow up.*

Yes, these are action verbs. But the actions they describe are too vague to be helpful when you're ready to do something. What if I said to you, "You've got five minutes until your next appointment—organize the staff meeting." You'd look at me in confusion, right? What are you supposed to do with that? Now imagine that I said to you, "You've got five minutes until your next appointment—reserve the conference room for the next staff meeting." You can do something speedy like that!

This doesn't mean that you should never use verbs like *organize*. In fact, there's a great place for them: your Projects list. The names of your Projects will probably not be immediately actionable, and use verbs like *plan*, *develop*, and *implement*. But it's essential to break those Projects down into Next Actions your doer will immediately understand, such as *call*, *draft*, and *email*.

Making each item on your list as specific as it can be doesn't take long once you get used to it. And it helps your doer work a lot faster and smarter. When it's time to move each action on your brain dump list into your task manager, keep these tips in mind.

Set Realistic Due Dates

If you've identified the correct category for each item on your brain dump list, and you now know how to rephrase it to inspire action, you may realize that some of your lists are longer than others. In fact, when people begin implementing the Empowered Productivity system, they often tell me that they have somewhere between 50 and 150 items on their Next Actions list. With that many items on your list, how do you avoid the Lion Syndrome? How can you quickly and easily choose the item on your list that is the best use of your time in that moment?

You need to add a second layer of organization. The first layer is categorical, using the specific categories described above. The second layer is organizing by time.

For each item on your list, ask yourself one question: "Given everything I need to do (everything on my task list and my calendar), what seems like a realistic date to get this one done?" The answer to this question will be the due date of the task. Then you'll sort each of your categories by date, in ascending order (soonest due date at the top, latest due date at the bottom).

By definition, *all* items on your task list have a weak relationship to time (because if they were happening on a certain day or time, they would be on your calendar). But some of your tasks will have an external due date that will help you to prioritize them (like the expense report that's due by the tenth of every month). In other cases, you'll need to assign your due date based on your priorities. For example, let's say today is Monday, and as I review my task list, I think, *I really need to email the client to check in on the proposal soon, but the website changes can wait*. In that case, you might make the due date Tuesday on the Next Action *Call the client*, and Friday on the Next Action *Add the new images to the home page of the website*.

You can use your discretion on due dates for actions in your other task categories. For example, items in your Future category may not need a due date, but you might want to set an alert to pop up around the time you think you need to make it current. In the example we used previously, it's August, and you want to hire a new employee before the end of the first quarter. An alert sometime in early December will prompt you to change the category on that item from Future to Projects, with a due date of March 31, and start creating Next Actions items with due dates to move that project forward.

When adding due dates to your tasks, you might discover that you've assigned yourself forty-seven things that are due tomorrow. As much as you might *want* them to happen tomorrow, when you see everything in black-and-white, you realize it's just not going to happen. So you'll need to spread your due dates out more realistically over the coming days and weeks. You might even need to recategorize some things as Future or Someday/Maybe.

In working with clients for decades, I've discovered that most people complete, on average, about three things from their Next Actions list per day. I know, that doesn't sound like enough! And, of course, you'll do many, many other things in the course of your day. But most of them will never even make it on your list because they involve those other demands on your time that invariably emerge, such as impromptu conversations, new incoming communications that contain more pressing task requests, all the meetings you have to attend daily, all of that incoming communication you need to stay on top of, and quick-turnaround assignments your boss drops on you without warning.

When you plan for only three Next Actions per day, your timelines will be more realistic, you'll be more informed about where you need to get more help or renegotiate timelines, there will be space to accommodate new priorities that do go on your list, and you can better cope with any crises that pop up without your plans going completely off the rails.

Crisis Management

Crises are unanticipated changes to your schedule and your priorities for the day or the week. They can be serious, like a parent's sudden illness, or minor, like a fender bender on the way to work. Let's face it: We don't have a crystal ball, so these unanticipated items come up *all the time.*

The best way to handle crises is to have the flexibility in your schedule to absorb them. If your calendar is stuffed back-to-back with appointments, meetings, and commitments, then you have no room for a crisis. A full calendar combined with an unexpected situation causes your plans to topple like dominoes.

Leaving some room in your calendar offers you two benefits. First, your day or week can absorb a crisis without too much disruption, making it much more manageable and perhaps not even a crisis at all. Second, whenever you don't have an unexpected situation, crisis, or changing priority, that room in your calendar provides the opportunity to get more things done and be proactive. In other words, when 80 percent or 90 percent of your week is committed to other things, not only will you be unable to absorb a crisis, you are leaving yourself no time to be proactive.

A good general rule is scheduling no more than 60 percent of your productive time—that is, the time you are awake and taking action. For example, my productive time begins around 7:00 a.m. I'm up and about, checking the weather, and gathering my belongings for the day. My productive time ends around 8:00 p.m., when I start relaxing and unwinding.

If you have work or personal commitments on your calendar that take up more than 60 percent of your productive time weekly, you are probably overcommitted. You don't have time to be proactive, and any crisis is likely to upend your life.

For you, 60 percent might not be exactly the right percentage, but it's a good starting point. You can do this whether you work nine-to-five at an office or are self-employed. If you share calendars with coworkers, protect some hours from having a meeting added. Limit your commitments to 60 percent of your productive time and see how your week goes. Are you being more proactive? More productive? Feeling less stressed? Dealing better with changing priorities? Adjust your percentage split accordingly.

FIVE

CHOOSE YOUR PRODUCTIVITY TOOLS

|||||||||||||||||||||||||||||||||||||||||||||||||||||||||||||||

As you've read this book and followed the instructions, you may have had questions about where you would ultimately be storing and managing your tasks. This chapter will answer those questions.

Like millions of other people, I used to rely on paper tools to organize my work. I lugged around a huge paper-based planner inside a zippered leather binder. As I write this book, paper planners are enjoying a bit of a resurgence. But, ultimately, I believe that paper planners will always place a distant second to great digital apps and software **plus** the methodology for using them to their ultimate benefit.

Around the year 2000, I reluctantly made the switch from my beloved paper planner to digital tools. I knew this was where the business world was headed, and I wanted to be prepared to teach my clients. The switch was hard, as I figured out how to transfer my behaviors into these digital tools. But once the process was completed, I quickly realized that apps and software dramatically increased my productivity and efficiency. Paper just couldn't compete anymore. And the good news is that you don't have to go through the hard part that I did, because the steps are all spelled out for you in this book!

Using paper planners might be a habit for some, but they simply aren't as efficient as digital tools, and you'll spend more time and effort if you try to manage the details of your life on paper. Here are the most important reasons why:

▸ *You can't back up a paper planner the way you can a digital tool.*

▸ *It's too easy to ignore a paper list amid the distractions from our various screens.*

▸ *You have to remember to take a paper planner with you. But since your phone is probably always with you, so are your digital productivity tools.*

▸ *A paper planner is bigger and heavier to carry around.*

▸ *It's easier to search digital tools.*

▸ *It's much faster (and neater) to change due dates, shuffle priorities, assign categories, and manage other details about your tasks and responsibilities using digital tools.*

▸ *Digital tools can send you reminders.*

▸ *You can share information (such as your schedule) with others faster and easier with digital tools than paper.*

▸ *Digital tools can store your completed actions, so you have an organized record of your accomplishments.*

▸ *Most paper tools are still centered on calendars, but you have more task items than calendar items, and task items are more efficiently organized categorically than by time.*

For all of these reasons, I strongly believe that digital tools are the most productive and efficient way to keep up with the demands of our busy lives in the twenty-first century. After deciding you can part with your paper, your will need to select the digital productivity tools you want to use. There are a lot of options out there, so I want to give you some criteria to help you make the best choices for you.

The Three Tools You Need

In order to fulfill the methodologies we have outlined thus far, you need three primary tools:

1 **Calendar**—as you learned earlier in this section, your calendar is for managing actions that have a strong relationship to time, like meetings and appointments.

2. **Task Manager**—here's where you'll manage your actions that have a weak relationship to time—in other words, the stuff that you work on between the commitments on your calendar. As you may have realized from reading this book, you can increase your productivity simply by the way you organize and write your to-do list.

3. **Notes**—any of those leftover items on your brain dump list that I discussed on page 77—those items that don't require action but will make it easier for you to take required actions in the future—are notes, and you need a place to store them. When choosing your tools, you should consider the platform(s) of your devices. For example, if you have all Apple devices, Microsoft tools may be more difficult to use than necessary. It's helpful if your tools are made specifically for your devices, and sync seamlessly to each device via the cloud.

Finally there are a few specific features required for your calendar tool and your task manager:

- **Calendar**—*your calendar tool should be able to send you alerts and reminders. It should also allow you to select different colors for different types of events.*

- **Task Manager**—*the tool you use for your task list must allow you to create your own categories, to set a due date* **and** *a reminder date, and to view your tasks in a variety of different ways (such as by project, by category, or by due date). It should allow you to easily search tasks, view completed tasks, and add comments and even documents to tasks. Lastly, your reminders (alerts) need to appear as push notifications on your devices (as opposed to showing up only when your app is open on your computer).*

- **Notes Manager**—*your notes tool should be easily accessible from all your devices, it should accept* *not only text notes but images, audio files, video files, and web clippings, and as a bonus, could have a feature that turns handwritten notes and words in images into searchable text.*

The bottom line is that your tools must have enough features to handle the complexity of your busy life, but not be so complicated that they feel like a burden. If you're used to using paper, you should expect a learning curve for digital tools. But once you've learned how to use them, they should feel fully integrated into your workflow, not like a separate and additional process you have to worry about. Tools that feel like just one more thing to manage are not the ones for you. The right tools feel logical and useful, and they inspire you to act.

My Recommendations for Productivity Tools

Most people already use some sort of digital calendar, contact manager, and email tools. If you like what you're using, and they have the features you need to support the action management behaviors you learned in this book, there's no reason to switch. For these three components, there isn't much difference between Outlook for Windows or Mac; Apple's productivity suite of Calendar, Contacts, and Mail; or Google's suite of Calendar, Contacts, and Gmail.

In my experience, most people have questions about tools for notes and tasks. Everyone's situation is different, but below I offer general recommendations, and the information above and at my website should help you make the best decision for your situation.

For notes, a very popular app with a lot of features is Evernote. But if you really like to handwrite, draw, or sketch with a stylus or Apple Pencil, consider Nebo. If you're steeped in Windows, you might prefer OneNote, as it's part of the Microsoft Office ecosystem.

Give the most consideration to the most important tool of your system: your task manager. If you already use Microsoft Outlook for Windows, the Tasks feature is robust. The Tasks feature in Outlook for Mac is lacking, and as of this writing I don't recommend it.

My overall recommendation for the best task manager is Todoist. If you are an Outlook for Windows user, it's a good option to consider going outside of Outlook to manage your tasks if you use an Apple iPhone and/or iPad. If you use Outlook for Mac, I absolutely recommend going outside of Outlook to manage your tasks and adding Todoist to your system.

If you use Google for your calendar, email, and contacts, I also recommend Todoist for tasks.

No matter what tools you choose, you'll get the most out of them if you take the time to learn their features. You can download detailed instructions for setting up and using both Todoist and the Tasks feature in Outlook for Windows with the Empowered Productivity system, plus images of sample task lists, at maurathomas.com/tools. With time, my recommendations for digital tools may change, so I'll continue to update that page and add to it any tools I might recommend in the future.

SIX

WORK YOUR SYSTEM, AND YOUR SYSTEM WILL WORK FOR YOU

Pat yourself on the back for creating a system that works for you and your productivity! There are just a few more things you need to know about how to keep it operating smoothly and supporting your productivity.

Capturing Your Thoughts

Remember, your set of tools is your one-stop resource for managing your work and your life. That means it's imperative to keep on channeling everything into your tools (your task list especially). One of the most critical habits to build is keeping everything you need to do out of your mind and into your tools.

Ideas, responsibilities, and other important thoughts will pop into your head unbidden. You can still jot them down on sticky notes, business cards, napkins, or anything else that's handy. But those random notes must find their way back to your single, central system. For example, I keep a pad of sticky notes beside my bed. When I wake up in the middle of the night, thinking of something I need to do, I don't want to have to turn on a device to access my task list. Instead, I scribble a note to myself in the dark and then enter it on my task list in the morning. When driving, I use my Bluetooth to instruct my device to email myself with the thought I have.

Of course, there are plenty of other options for capturing information on the go, starting with the mobile versions of your productivity tools. While your desktop is the best place for doing deep work with your system, you should know how to use your devices to create a task or enter other information.

The Weekly Update

Any system needs regular maintenance to stay functional. I recommend maintenance that I call **the Weekly Update**. This is a routine check-in that keeps you on track with your commitments, communication, and information. You will make frequent updates to your list daily as events unfold, but an intentional review every week is also important.

Friday is a good time to do your Weekly Update. I suggest you make it a recurring appointment on your calendar. When you first start using the Empowered Productivity system, your Weekly Update might take 45 minutes to an hour to complete. But the more practice you get with this process, the faster your update will go. Mine takes only a few minutes each week. The time you invest in the Weekly Update pays off many times over in peace of mind, efficiency, and focus.

To complete your weekly update, follow these steps.

1 **Review tasks.** Scan all of your tasks for adjustments and updates required, such as overdue items, tasks you've completed but forgot to check off, Projects that need a Next Action identified. About once a quarter, scan your Future and Someday/Maybe lists to see whether anything should be moved to active.

2 **Do a brain dump and a roundup.** We got everything out of your head earlier, but if you're not diligent, it's going to fill right back up again. That's why it's important to "download" those thoughts from your brain weekly and get everything into your tools. After you make your initial list, review it against the brain dump prompts on page 17 to ensure that you've truly captured everything. Also take a moment to round up any notes and reminders you've left for yourself in other places and get them into your tools.

3. **Look back.** Review your calendar for the week that's ending. Have you closed all the loops? Are there any action items you should add to your system based on things that happened this week?

4. **Look ahead.** Review your upcoming calendar to ensure that you have no surprises in the coming week and that you are prepared, or have plans to be prepared, for every event.

After you complete your weekly update every Friday, you'll be able to enter your weekend without nagging worries about your responsibilities clouding your mind. That helps you give your full attention to the people you care about and the activities you need for rest and relaxation. When you can enjoy this restorative time without feeling tethered to the office, you'll be at your best when work rolls around again on Monday.

CONCLUSION

YOU'RE BACK IN THE DRIVER'S SEAT NOW

Dwight D. Eisenhower has been credited with saying, "What is important is seldom urgent and what is urgent is seldom important." Apparently he was notorious for applying this to the prioritization of his workload. Even in Eisenhower's day, productivity students recognized the value of this wisdom and developed the Eisenhower Matrix. Decades later, Stephen R. Covey adapted it in *The 7 Habits of Highly Effective People*, where he called it the Four Quadrants.

The Eisenhower Matrix considers all demands on your attention in terms of only two factors: importance and urgency. The top axis measures importance from low to high, and the side axis measures urgency from least urgent to most urgent.

The work you've done setting up your productivity tools will help you deal with each quadrant effectively:

▸ **Low importance, low urgency.** *Even though actions in this quadrant won't affect your life in a huge way, they can still weigh on your mind. By getting them out of your head during your brain dump, you can now devote your mental energy to other things. Using location as a category on your task list helps keep these tasks off your mind until you're somewhere that you can act on them. For example, your task list won't stress you out at work by reminding you of all the things you want to work on at home. And learning to assign realistic due dates gives you a clearer sense of when you might actually get around to these tasks.*

Perhaps that led you to take some of them off your list entirely, move them to your Future or Someday/Maybe category, or hire help to complete them.

▷ **Low importance, high urgency.** *It's tempting to work on each demand for your attention as it arrives. But while those demands—your full inbox, your pinging phone, the coworker headed for your desk— feel pressing, they're usually not related to the things you most need to accomplish. When you don't have a clear sense of your own priorities, you're more likely to just go along with how other people want you to spend your time. But now that you have all of your commitments captured on your calendar and task list, you can better set your own priorities, while still remaining responsive to others. You go from reactive to proactive.*

▷ **High importance, high urgency.** *In this quadrant are the high-impact, time-sensitive tasks that often arise* suddenly. For example, your boss assigns you a task that must be done by the end of the day. Or your kids come down with a nasty bug, so you need to make doctor appointments, reschedule some meetings, and cancel your family's weekend plans. Using your new productivity system, you now know to leave room in your schedule for the unexpected. You can quickly reprioritize without letting any of your other tasks fall through the cracks.

▸ **High importance, low urgency.** Your big picture goals are in this quadrant. These goals include your deepest personal aspirations like launching your own business, going back to school, starting a family, running for office, writing a book, or taking an extended trip abroad. They also include work projects that are close to your heart—for example, creating a new service offering, launching a mentor-ship program, landing a promotion, or speaking at the top conference in your field. Lastly, they include *the big picture activities that you were hired for in the first place—the main components of your job description. Because there's no external deadline on the items in this quadrant, it's all too easy to let them fall off your radar and never accomplish them. But now you can feel confident that your task list has captured these goals and will remind you of them. And with your other quadrants under control, you have less mental clutter and more room for your creativity to flow. You free up the space to make happen what's most important.*

President Eisenhower would be proud of you: You're managing your attention in each of the four quadrants. You're making real progress on what's important to you. You're notching more wins every day. And each win motivates you and energizes you to achieve more.

ACKNOWLEDGMENTS

At the start of my professional career, I had the honor of working at a company called Time/Design with productivity legend David Allen. This was many years before *Getting Things Done* was published, and he was delivering training that I learned as "the Time/Design process." Some of what I learned of the Time/Design process is incorporated into this action management portion of my Empowered Productivity series. And much of what I knew as the Time/Design process was also published in David's book, *Getting Things Done*, becoming part of the GTD methodology. The similarities between Empowered Productivity and Getting Things Done have their roots in what I learned

FROM TO-DO TO DONE

during my time at Time/Design. I feel fortunate to have received the early part of my education in productivity from both Mr. Allen and Time/Design.

This book would not be possible without the great team at Sourcebooks, and especially my dedicated editor, Meg Gibbons. Thank you for being my partner in this process! I also need to thank my mom, Rita Kerins, and my husband, Shawn Thomas, who are always my first readers. Your dedication, support, and guidance mean everything to me.

ABOUT THE AUTHOR

 **Maura Nevel Thomas** is an award-winning international speaker, trainer, and author on individual and corporate productivity and work-life balance, and she is the most widely cited authority on attention management.

She helps driven, motivated knowledge workers control their attention and regain control over the details of their life and work. Maura has trained over forty thousand individuals at over two thousand organizations on her proprietary Empowered Productivity system, a process for achieving significant results and living a life of choice.

Maura's clients include the likes of Dell, Old Navy, the U.S. Army, L'Oréal, the American Heart Association, NASA's Johnson Space Center, and Adobe. She is a TEDx speaker, successful entrepreneur, a certified speaking professional from the National Speakers Association, and author of *Personal Productivity Secrets*, *Work Without Walls*, and *Attention Management*. She is a media favorite, featured regularly in a variety of national business outlets, including the *Wall Street Journal*, NPR, *Fast Company*, *Entrepreneur*, *U.S. News & World Report*, and the *Huffington Post*. She is also a regular contributor to both *Forbes* and the *Harvard Business Review*, with articles there viewed over a million times.

Maura earned an MBA from the Isenberg School of Management at the University of Massachusetts and has studied the field of productivity all over the world for more than two decades.

Maura believes that every person has unique gifts to offer the world, and her purpose is to support them in offering those gifts in a way that is joyful and inspiring. She strives to have an impact that is relevant and unique, presenting new ideas and ways of thinking that are applicable to changing times.

Social impact is very important to Maura, so she is very active in her local community of Austin, Texas, where she has held volunteer leadership and mentor positions in a variety of different community organizations and charities. This belief also leads Maura to offer quarterly pro-bono presentations to nonprofits, to donate a percentage of all her revenues to charity, and to have volunteered as a Climate Project speaker (personally trained on the subject by former vice president and Nobel laureate Al Gore and his team of leading climate scientists).

NEW! Only from Simple Truths®

spark impact in just one hour

IGNITE READS IS A NEW SERIES OF 1-HOUR READS WRITTEN BY WORLD-RENOWNED EXPERTS!

These captivating books will help you become the best version of yourself, allowing for new opportunities in your personal and professional life. Accelerate your career and expand your knowledge with these powerful books written on today's hottest ideas.

TRENDING BUSINESS AND PERSONAL GROWTH TOPICS

 Read in an hour or less

 Leading experts and authors

 Bold design and captivating content

EXCLUSIVELY AVAILABLE ON SIMPLETRUTHS.COM

Need a training framework?
Engage your team with discussion guides and PowerPoints for training events or meetings.

Want your own branded editions?
Express gratitude, appreciation, and instill positive perceptions to staff or clients by adding your organization's logo to your edition of the book.

Add a supplemental visual experience
to any meeting, training, or event.

Contact us for special corporate discounts!
(800) 900-3427 x247 or
simpletruths@sourcebooks.com

LOVED WHAT YOU READ AND WANT MORE?

Sign up today and be the FIRST to receive advance copies of Simple Truths® NEW releases written and signed by expert authors. Enjoy a complete package of supplemental materials that can help you host or lead a successful event. This high-value program will uplift you to be the best version of yourself!

— SIMPLE TRUTHS —
ELITE CLUB
ONE MONTH. ONE BOOK. ONE HOUR.

Your monthly dose of motivation, inspiration, and personal growth.